THE MOUNTAIN
KEEPS ITS OWN TIME

THE MOUNTAIN KEEPS ITS OWN TIME

POEMS AND PHOTOGRAPHS FROM WESTERN NORTH CAROLINA

Joe Beckham

Photographs by Skip Sickler

Faraway Publishing
Black Mountain, N.C.

The author may be contacted at
28 Wagon Trail, Unit 313
Black Mountain, NC 28711
joebeckham311@gmail.com

The photographer may be contacted at
1216 Land Harbor
Newland, NC 28657
skiplisa1@bellsouth.net

Published by
FARAWAY PUBLISHING
125 Spring View Drive
Black Mountain, N.C. 28711
farawaypublishing@gmail.com

ISBN: 979-8-9990731-4-3 (pbk.)
Library of Congress Control Number: 2026940015

Printed in the United States of America
10 9 8 7 6 5 4 3 2 1
All Photographs by Burton H. Sickler, Jr., except White Horse photograph, courtesy of White Horse, North Carolina, and Looking Glass Mountain by Joe Beckham.

To the people of western Carolina,
whose courage, resilience, and optimism
have been a source of inspiration.

The mountain keeps time in slips, in moss,
in the quiet undoing of edges.
— A. R. Ammons

CONTENTS

Preface xi

Acknowledgments xiii

Accidental Meditation 1

Cemetery 3

Copperhead 6

Helene 8

Neighbors 11

Herons 13

The House at Grassy Branch 15

Impermanence 18

In the Museum 21

Lost and Found 23

Memento Mori 26

Advice 28

Linville Falls 30

Being Mortal 32

Belay 34

Black Hole 36

Late Summer, Craggy Branch 38

Interval 40

The Meaning of Life 42

Red-Tailed Hawk 44

Evening Gathers at the White Horse 46

The Goldfinch 48

Cardinals 51

Country Dancing 52

Morning News 54

Mt. Mitchell, After Helene 57

Night Road, Blue Ridge 61

On the Porch 63

Possible Selves 66

Morning Contemplation 68

An Ordinary Moment 70

Presence..72
Roan Mountain...73
Fate in Flight...76
Climbing Looking Glass...79
The French Broad River...81
French Broad in Spring..84
French Broad in Summer..85
French Broad in Fall..86
French Broad in Winter..87
Light Moving Through Current..................................88
Little Tennessee Greenway...90
Self-Improvement, Asheville Style.............................92
Quieting the Inner Voice...95
Table Rock, Second Pitch..97
Five Falls, Chattooga River..99
Faithful to What Endures..102
Backyard Oak...105
Serial Killer, Blue Ridge..107
Bluebird at the Door...110
What Remains...113
Memories Still Warm..115
I Do Not Grieve for Summer...................................118
Nature's Lesson...120
80th Birthday...122
Anything Left to Say?..123
About the Author..126
About the Photographer..127

PREFACE

This book began, as many things do, without announcement.

Not as a project, not even as a collection, but as a habit of paying attention—of walking the ridges and riverbanks of western North Carolina and trying, in language, to keep pace with what was already there. A line would come on a trail. Another while standing at a river's edge. Sometimes a phrase arrived uninvited, like fog lifting just enough to reveal the next turn. Over time, these moments accumulated into poems, and the poems—quietly, without insistence—became this book.

I did not set out to write *The Mountain Keeps Its Own Time*. The title arrived much later, when it became clear that what drew me back, again and again, was not simply the landscape but the way it resists our urgency. In these mountains, time is not something we manage. It is something we enter. The rivers move whether or not we understand them. The light changes without consulting us. Even loss—of trees, of seasons, of people—unfolds on a scale that humbles explanation.

My motivations for writing these poems are both simple and difficult to name. I wanted to see more clearly. I wanted to remember what I might otherwise pass by. And perhaps most of all, I wanted to place human experience—our small rituals, our anxieties, our brief moments of clarity—within a larger field where they might be held, if not resolved.

The photographs included here grew out of the same impulse. They are not illustrations of the poems, nor are the poems captions for the images. Rather, they are parallel ways of noticing—two forms of attention moving through the same terrain. At times they intersect. At times they diverge. Together, I hope they offer a fuller sense of place.

The writing of this book was not without its challenges. The most persistent was learning what to leave out. The landscape invites

description but resists excess. Early drafts often tried to say too much—
to explain what the mountains already understood without language.
Over time, I found myself drawn toward compression, toward a quieter
line that allows space for the reader to enter.

There were other challenges as well. To write honestly about this
region required acknowledging not only its beauty but its
vulnerability—storms that reshape entire valleys, forests altered by
forces both natural and human, communities that endure and adapt.
Holding that balance—between reverence and clarity, between
attention and restraint—became an essential part of the work.

In the end, this book is less a statement than a record of listening.

If these poems succeed, it is not because they capture the
mountains but because they point, however briefly, toward what
cannot be held: the movement of water over stone, the shift of light
along a ridge, the sense—felt but not fully named—that we are part of
something both fleeting and continuous.

The mountains keep their own time.

These pages are my attempt to notice.

Joe Beckham
Black Mountain, N.C.
May, 2026

ACKNOWLEDGMENTS

My life as a poet began, though I did not yet know it, during a summer, working as a fishing guide in Yellowstone National Park, and continued through my years as an instructor with Outward Bound in North Carolina, Minnesota, and Hurricane Island. A poetry workshop at the University of Florida in the 1960s led me to begin recording reflections on these outdoor experiences. Those early journals have remained a wellspring for much of what I write.

After retiring from a forty-year academic career, I returned to the mountains of Western North Carolina—first to Asheville and ultimately to Black Mountain, where I have made my final home. Along the way, I have been fortunate to receive encouragement and guidance from generous readers and friends. I am especially grateful to John Calderazzo and Ben Brown, who recognized something in my early efforts and helped me take the work more seriously.

Here in North Carolina, I found a sustaining community through the Osher Lifelong Learning Institute at the University of North Carolina Asheville. The Second Friday and Third Friday groups at OLLI have offered thoughtful critique and steady companionship, and I have learned deeply from fellow poets in those circles. I am particularly grateful to Mary Louisa Ippolito and Adriana de Kanter for their contributions. I also appreciate the workshops offered through OLLI, especially the guidance of Jay Jacoby, whose work with advanced students helped me find a more confident voice.

Beyond OLLI, I have been fortunate to be part of a vibrant community of poets in Black Mountain, including Lauren Yoder and others whose dedication to the craft continues to inspire me.

I am deeply grateful to my editor and publisher, Randolph Shaffner, for his steady guidance and collaboration throughout the process of writing, editing, and bringing this book into the world. My co-conspirator, Skip Sickler, has been an essential partner, contributing both his photographs of western North Carolina and his enduring enthusiasm for the project, rooted in his own connection to Outward Bound.

Finally, I thank Margo Nottoli, Sara Sterling, and my daughter, Sofie Beckham, for their constant encouragement and support along the way.

ACCIDENTAL MEDITATION

Reviewing the small tasks of the day,
I paused at a window,
watching rain stitch the valley together
with threads silvered in morning light.

Sourwoods in the field
held their thin branches to the wind,
still remembering
the evening's storm.

When they swayed,
my arms answered—
as if the same plea
moved through bark to bone

A split-rail fence sagged beyond the grass,
its rails made frail by years of weather.

Beyond it, ridges folded
in their winter blue,
one behind another
like quilts hung out to air.

Fog rose from the cove below
and pooled among the trees,
filling as cream fills a bowl,
until birches stood knee-deep in whiteness
and rhododendron tunnels disappeared.

It did not lift but thickened, settled deeper,
softening fence lines, stones,
even the far ridge,
until distance
closed its eyes.

I stayed there
in the same white hush,
as if the mountain
had taken me into itself
and the earth had drawn a blanket
over restless ground.

CEMETERY

I wander through the cemetery,
as though I were people-watching the dead.
Pausing at each stone
like a tourist of finished lives.

Here the graves lean downhill;
perhaps they're listening
to traffic on Charlotte Street;
a faint tide of engines
rises through the trees.

Moss has taken the north sides,
thick as an old sweater,
softening the names.
Some people are anonymous
to everyone but lichen.

A plastic bouquet has faded
to a color no flower ever was.
A real fern grows beside it,
doing a better job.

Between the dates
a small Appalachian dash,
no bigger than a scratch
a briar might leave on your wrist.
It holds floods and droughts,
mill layoffs, long drives on I-40,
the winter the power went out
and everyone learned again
how quiet night can be.

Someone here must have known
the smell of rain
rising off hot asphalt
after a storm rolled down
from the Pisgah,
must have stood on a porch,
watching lightning walk Mitchell's ridges.

I read the stones
like name tags
no one is networking.
Trying to reverse-engineer
an entire biography
from typography.

I brush pine needles
off a low marker.
A courtesy

to someone who can't return it.
I step carefully between plots
so as not to wake anyone.

Not because I believe they would,
but because it feels rude
to walk loudly
through a space
where so many lives
have gone quiet.

Someday I'll be here too,
my years trimmed down

To the same efficient formatting.
My decades compressed
so that whoever pauses at my stone
will never suspect
an excellent story
is missing.

COPPERHEAD

I stepped over a copperhead
lying in the leaf-brown grammar of the trail—
quiet as an unspoken sentence.

Grey-brown hourglass bands,
narrowing, widening—
careful punctuation.

Its snout pressed
against a stone—
testing for an edge.

Then—
the old life loosened.

A thin brightness moved beneath,
a hidden river finding forward.
The eyes, once clouded,
cleared.

I stood still,
aware of something similar
working in me
without a name.

How long had a new self
waited just beneath—
patient as roots under clay?

The snake moved on,
leaving an emptied shell
turned inside out,

light as a memory
already loosening.

A quiet slipping free.

You go on,
not entirely sure
what has fallen away,
only that it no longer fits.

On the trail—
the outline
of who you were.
Something you needed,
something that carried you,

now light enough
to leave
to the leaves.

HELENE

Water pulses over asphalt.
Under the asphalt, red clay;
under the clay, roots gripping stone;
under the stones, pressure
older than the hills.

Trees collapsing power lines,
roads unlearning
where they were meant to go,
the careful scaffolding of habit
undone in a surging tempest.

We step outside,
calling out for one another—
not because we are brave
but because someone calls
and we answer.

Answering
Is how life begins again.

Somewhere, a chainsaw starts,
stops, starts again.
Someone climbs a ladder,
tacking tin over a torn roof.
A candle burns
for one
who has not come home.

Nothing is guaranteed:
not the Parkway staying put,

not the French Broad keeping its banks,
not tomorrow's light.

Everything is given
moment by moment,
like water
poured into cupped hands.

The world leans close
each day
to see whether we will answer
with fear
or fortitude.

The quiet agreement to go on
makes us human—
moving toward light,
moving toward one another
when the lights go out.

Morning returns slowly.
Mist lifts from the coves.
Light rinses the surfaces of things.

Birds rehearse their surprise
that anything remains.

And the day steps forward
like a deer from the trees—
ready to vanish,
yet willing, for this moment,
to eat from our hands.

87 River Road

NEIGHBORS

After the storm,
our neighbors
came to visit.

They listened
as a field listens—
grass bending,
from its long conversation
with wind.

They did not stand above the world.
They entered it
as water enters soil,
finding what opens.

There was a steadiness in them,
like a stone warmed all day in sun,
held easily in the hand.

They laughed
when hidden threads appeared—
this grief tied to that joy,
this loss already flowering.

Ask them what is right:
they paused
long enough
for the answer
to arrive.

A cup placed
where a hand will find it.
A word that does not bruise.
Silence, when silence heals.

After the storm
there was a widening—
as when dusk
takes the day into itself
without argument,

And everything
that had been scattered
began, quietly,
to gather.

HERONS

The blue-grey form waits
at the pond's edge—
a stillness in the reeds,
shouldering February's chill.

A pulse below the black water.
Neck stiffens, stretches, spears,
and swallows.

Lifting, it rows through air,
slow wings beating,
nothing wasted.

Settling again
where grass sways
along the far bank;
others arrive—

independent hunters,
aware only faintly
of one another.

Their legs stir in the shallows.
Shadows lengthen
in the quickening dusk.

THE HOUSE AT GRASSY BRANCH

After the loss
that loosened my footing,
there was a house
already practiced in living.

My daughter's children
had grown there.
The rooms
still held
the shape of their voices.

Two sides opened to forest
rising to the ridge.
The Parkway's green corridor
passed nearby,
a migration route
the mountains kept watch over.

A sow and her cubs
climbed apple trees,
their weight shaking green fruit,
thudding softly in the grass.

Deer came evenings
to consider the roses
until the garden taught me
which plants survive appetite.

Spring kept my knees in the soil
weeding among
hydrangea, butterfly weed,

coneflower, black-eyed Susan,
small suns
opening in the air.

Summer gathered us
into outdoor games,
while river birch and tulip poplar
shifted their leaves
in mountain light.

Autumn deepened the ridges.
Friends leaned close to the fire.
Children ran through dusk
while sparks drifted upward
into the patient dark.

Something quiet moved
through those days—
like light shifting
through moving water.

Three and a half years
passed like weather
crossing the mountains.

Some things remain.

Like seeds caught
in the cuff of a pant leg,
they travel with me
the rest of the way.

IMPERMANENCE

When young,
no announcement came:
loss worked the way weather does,
crossing the Blue Ridge at night,
leaving the towns below
to wake and name it.

It did not arrive all at once
but rehearsed in smaller roles—
a friend's empty desk,
silver working into your father's hair,
the dog sleeping longer,
running in dreams
through a field
you could no longer enter.

Years later this proved useful.
Fever breaks on its own timetable.
Shame eventually tires of its voice.
Snow withdraws its white argument
from pasture and fence post,
leaving the ground to speak again.

Still, something in us
wants a road that will hold.
We say "always"
as if the word were a spike
driven through sky into stone.

Yet the mountains are lowering
grain by grain
into the French Broad.
Old barns fold politely

into their shadows.
Hemlocks stand gray and thinning.

Impermanence leans close
even in the hour of joy,
like a neighbor on the porch
who never knocks
and won't leave.
The earth turns
like a mill wheel
when water insists.
Fog lifts, returns, lifts again,
the ridge practicing
how to disappear.

Forever, infinity—
words like empty mason jars
on a pantry shelf.
We store our days in them anyway,
trusting a lid
no one has tested.

This morning
light found the kitchen table
without hesitation.
Coffee steamed.
Outside, a wren tried out its voice
against the cold air,
as if sound
might vanish.

I sat there listening,
not to keep anything,
only to be present
while it was given.

IN THE MUSEUM

I stood before daguerreotypes,
and a kindness rose in me
for lives I did not know.
The ache for a long-ago life.
Homesickness for a home I never knew.

Men and women captured
inside their own brief light,
hands folded, faces steady,
as if the day had asked them
to stand still.

Their world pressed itself upon them—
crossing streets of mud and manure,
walking on sidewalks of wooden plank.
Smoke and heat were stitched into cloth and hair,
the sweet and sour labor of being alive.

Their days exuded color.
Not the colors we preserve
but the ones that cling:
dust, damp wool,
green panic of summer illness,
blue ache of evening,
Iron smell of trains passing close.

Here I am, clean-handed,
vaccinated, buffered by glass,
leaning in as if proximity
could teach me something essential.

I borrow their gravity,
their seriousness of being.

This is what the museum gives us—
permission to feel tenderness
for time, for life,
for how it carries us—
then compels us
to imagine the rest.

LOST AND FOUND

Morning fog lifts
out of the cove
below the Blue Ridge Parkway.
It smells faintly
of leaf mold and stone.

A drop falls
from a hemlock branch
onto the back of my hand.
Cold enough to sting.

Somewhere down the slope,
water threads through mossed rock
toward the West Fork of the Pigeon.
I cannot see it,
but it keeps up
its patient talking.

The trail narrows
past the last white blaze.
Rhododendron closes overhead,
laurel snagging at sleeves.

A semi echoing up from Tunnel Road,
a wood thrush
ringing its hollow flute,
the soft scuff
of boots
on damp needles.

The path returns
as if it had stepped aside
until I calmed down.

On the ridge
wind combs the heads of little bluestem,
first one way,
then the other.

Mountains fade
toward Tennessee —
layer after layer
of blue haze
until distance becomes
a color, no longer a place.

Going back,
I feel accompanied,
as if the day itself
had walked beside me
like an old hiker
who knows these switchbacks
by heart
and does not ask
why I came.

MEMENTO MORI

Late at night
I stand where the road goes quiet
and the hills give back only a few lights
across the distance.

Each light could be someone laughing,
someone turning toward sleep,
someone staring out their window,
thinking this same thought.

While I'm wondering about them,
they might be wondering about me—
imagining what it's like to stand right here,
in this exact loneliness.

Once, I believed I could arrive everywhere,
but every step gently shuts a door.
The paths we choose
carry the weight
of all the paths refused.

At the end, if someone asked
what the world was like,
I'd say, "I lived in one small part of it,
learned the sound of its evenings,
and was grateful for the lights
that kept shining
after I turned away.

ADVICE

for Wyeth

I offer it
the way an old trail offers
direction—
worn by weather
and the weight of other feet.

Woods have shifted since then.
Storms felled trees.
Streams moved their crossings.
A ridge that once opened
now closed in laurel.

You walk
another version of the mountain.

So take what I say
as you might take
an outdated map—
useful mostly for knowing
someone passed this way
and was uncertain too.

Most of what I learned
was only
how little survived the crossing.

You are heading out
into a different landscape
with hills I have never climbed
and a wind
that will not recognize my name.

My advice will drift from you
the way fog lifts
from a morning valley.

What we call wisdom
is simply the sound
of one person
remembering how surprised
they were by their own life.

LINVILLE FALLS

for John Calderazzo

I went up through spruce as morning woke—
snow pooled in hollows,
mist loosening its thin veil.

At Linville Falls
the river pressed a channel through the gorge,
its voice a growl
finding a throat in stone.

I crouched at a ledge.
Cardinal flowers leaned into spray.
Lichen held to boulders
cooled by mist and shade.

Something in me answered—
not thought, but a lowering
into what listens.

My stride lengthened.
Weight tipped forward.
The body remembered its use.

In a clearing, dusk gathered.
Primrose opened.
Brambles held dark fruit—
tight clusters, thorn-guarded,
staining the ground.

I fed—juice, seed,
the insistence of hunger—
until night took me

and loosened the name
I had been given.

At dawn, warmth found my back.
Breath widened the ribs.
The world arrived as scent and motion—
shadows moving
without needing to be known.

Below, the river shouldered through stone.
I went to it,
lumbering—
as if the body had already chosen.

Certain now
of water,
of current,
of going on.

BEING MORTAL

for Maddie

We live on a short lease
with everything else—
the oak leaf browning on the lawn,
the snowbank shrinking
from the bottom up,
a cup of coffee cooling
while we talk.

No one tells us
what counts as a long time.
A summer can feel endless
until it is Labor Day,
and then it is a postcard
found years later
in a drawer.

Even the stars
are burning themselves out,
though from here
they look steady as porch lights
left on for someone
who isn't coming back.

So we do what people do.
We decide that one afternoon
matters more than another—
the day your granddaughter laughed
so hard she cried,
the day sunlight filled the living room
and every floating speck
seemed necessary.

Nothing about those hours
was longer than any other,
but they thickened in the heart,
like syrup on a spoon.

This is what being mortal allows:
to keep a few bright moments
in a safe place inside us,
taking them out carefully,
turning them in the light,
as if they might wear out.

And at the end—
which comes the way evening does,
gradually, without asking—
we lay them down again,
one by one,
on the bedside table of the world,
and switch off the lamp.

BELAY

A child falling asleep on your chest,
breathing small tides
of trust.

or a blue ridge road
after midnight,
wheel steady under your hands,
while behind you
a soft republic of sleeping friends
has surrendered
attention

or the faint weight
coming onto your anchor,
when the climber above
moves beyond the ledge—
and out of sight—

line tightening
through the brake
in your grip.

And it comes to you
not as pride
or fear
but with something unspoken
when the world
sometimes places
another life
in the open palm
of your hand,

the way gravity
simply assumes
the mountain
will hold the snow.

BLACK HOLE

Everything goes,
nothing returns.
Not that plastic container lid
or the sock lost in the drier.

Mass folded until
light fails to report back.
So dense
The future bends inward.

We knew it early—
dark at the bottom of basement stairs,
snorkeling cold ocean depths,
peering over a chasm on a mountain summit.

There is a thrill in feeling the ledge's tug,
leaning out, held by curiosity.
The body senses the balance:
inquiry versus survival.

Each step nearer the edge
is to feel the pull.
The problem is
you never know how close you are.

You think you've stepped back,
but maybe the universe
has quietly shifted
a few centimeters toward the abyss.

So we build railings, fences, norms, laws—
fragile agreements.
Yet sturdy enough

to keep bodies upright.

It may be healthy
to stare into the dark now and then—
to feel the pull
and step back

not entirely sure
what moved.

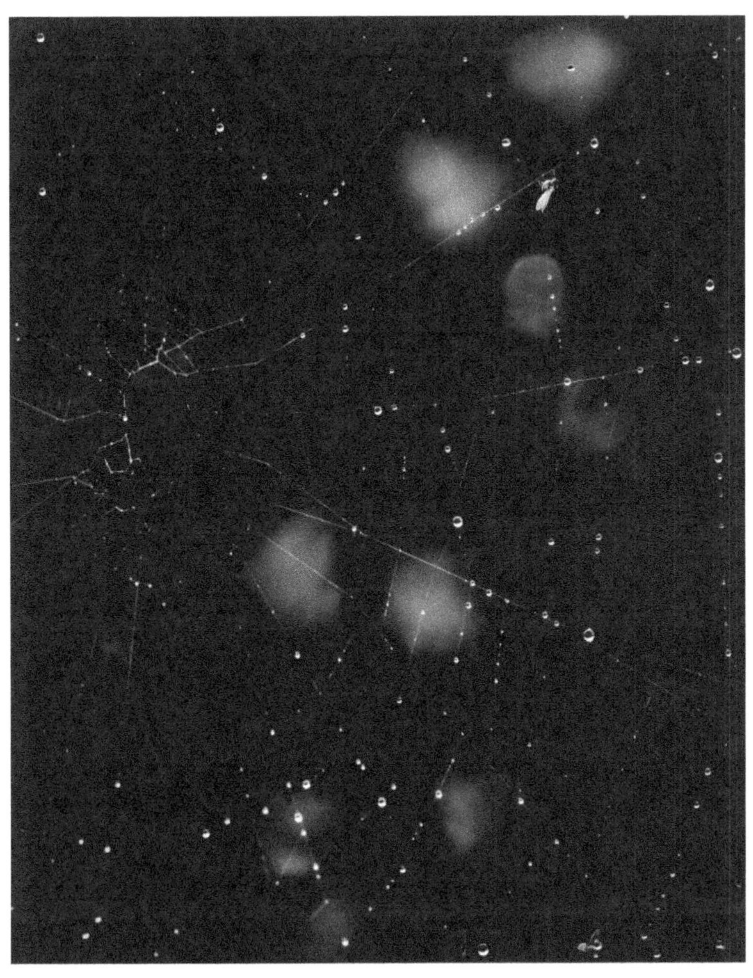

LATE SUMMER, CRAGGY BRANCH

By August the creek near Craggy Branch
has forgotten its voice.

What used to speak in steady sentences
now rests between stones—
a few clear words left
in the deeper places.

The rhododendron holds its leaves,
a promise it isn't sure it can keep.
The moss along the bank
has drawn back into itself.

The drought, they say,
and the year before that—
as if weather were something
you could stack neatly and put away.

The tulip poplar in the yard
lets go early now,
a leaf here, another there,
not in season,
not all at once—

just enough
to make you wonder
what it remembers
that the rain has not yet forgiven.

INTERVAL

Sometimes an event
arrives faster
than the spirit can receive it.

The mind lingers behind
on a Blue Ridge overlook
where the mountains fall away
in patient layers—

and something happens:

For a moment
nothing moves inside you.

The feeling
is still traveling
the long hollows of the body.

Lightning striking somewhere
beyond the spruce line—

that white instant
when the mountains
are briefly bones of light.

You wait
in the held breath of the valley

to hear
how close
the thunder
has come
to saying
your name.

THE MEANING OF LIFE

Perhaps enlightenment will reveal
nothing was hidden from us—
only that the question itself
has been moving for centuries
through these mountains,

wandering ridge to ridge,
slipping through coves and hollows
before anyone thinks to ask.

This morning the fog
was already at work in the valley,
loosening among birch and hemlock,
lifting a little at a time,
the day relearning
how to begin.

And I wondered—
if every question arrived solved,
if each day came
with its explanation attached,

would we still stop
beside a creek
to watch sunlight
work its grammar
across moving water—

or miss entirely
what the fog knows:

that meaning passes quietly
through the world,
touching leaf and stone and water
for a moment,
then moving on again
in the long conversation
between mountain and sky.

RED-TAILED HAWK

Complete
in the opening of its wings—

rising on what cannot be seen,
a lifting already there
before the body finds it.

Circling—
nothing added.

Air receives it
without question.

Above,
space opening into itself.

Below,
the field goes on—
seed heads loosening,
light crossing from blade to blade.

You stand here—
thoughts passing
like brief shadows in grass.

The hawk turns.
Its shadow turns.

No edge to follow.
No center to keep.

Only the widening arc.

EVENING GATHERS AT THE WHITE HORSE

Evening gathers at the White Horse door
as if it has a reservation.

Coats on a hook—
Patagonia, thrift store wool,
something that looks accidental.

Inside, the room offers warm light
from a lit stage,
faces leaning toward sound,
echoing a low murmur calibrated
to suggest anticipation.

Someone tunes a guitar
while a fiddle tries on an old accent—
a reel that crossed over
to this side of the Atlantic.

There is the banjo's *bum ditty*,
ever bright and insistent,
with a history
nobody here feels obligated to explain.

A mandolin picks something resonant
out of whatever's left of the day,
while a bass riffs a line
that vibrates in the inner ear.

We may have come for bluegrass velocity
or something adjacent—
for a Celtic echo
we're comfortable borrowing

without inheriting the weather
or a folk song carrying a history
of authenticity and social conscience.

Soon the music will begin.
Someone will dim the lights.
Someone will say *welcome*,
which is both invitation and absolution.

And then it happens—
the first notes rising
faster than intention,
a high, lonesome agreement
we enter without signing,
as if what brought us here
wasn't the long habit
of wanting to belong to something
that's been moving through these hills
long before we named it
and long after we forget.

THE GOLDFINCH

A small insistence of brightness
against the field's green.

Light enough
to hang from a thistle,
to trust the bending,
while seed by seed,
the thistle consents.

A brief lifting—
then the downward arc
as if the air itself
is a question it answers
by entering.

Something in you
tries to follow—
not the wing,
but the ease.

Swing and turn. Jubilee.

Its flight is not a line
but a going—
rise, fall,
a small agreement with air.

Swing and turn. Jubilee.

In winter
the brightness goes

without complaint.
Something quieter
continues.
And others gather—
keeping their own plan in the drift,
not as one,
but near enough.

Live and learn. Jubilee

You watch,
a stem bowed under weight
that is almost nothing,
the bird tipping it farther,
then righting—
a husk loosening,
falling through light
you can't quite see
until it turns—

Swing and turn. Jubilee

and the goldfinch
lifting, bright as a breath taken in,
leaving you there
with the field
still opening,
still giving.

Live and Learn. Jubilee

CARDINALS

On a blown barren bough
cardinals huddle,
feathers fluffed against the cold.
Snow veils the field,
burying the roots of river birch.
A fence stands in the distance,
the forest flowing beyond.
A branch falls:
the air is dusted with crimson.

COUNTRY DANCING

Dancing starts
in the small adjustments
you make
to avoid standing
like a person who has forgotten
what brought them here.

A heel taps.
A knee gives.
just keeping time—
nothing you'll have to explain later.

Then the music leans in,
a steady insistence.
The body answers
before your better judgment
can intervene.

A sway you could deny,
a turn that looks accidental.
Hands meet hands—
briefly,
without ambition.

Here in the mountains
It's a legacy:
Contra,
Square,
English Country.

Someone calls the next move,
so no one has to admit
they don't know what they're doing.

There's comfort in that—
the pattern carrying you
past the need to improvise,
and you stop managing it.

Each step remembers something—
a crossing, a turning,
a brief holding on
before letting go again.

People moving together
in time,
in place,
in a shared remembering
that reaches back
through generations—
and outward
into the living world around them.

MORNING NEWS

Ice somewhere loosens
its long memory of cold.
A forest learns
the language of fire.
Oceans warm themselves
like a fever no one
has the authority to treat.

Wars drift across continents.
Cities open into smoke.
Children carried through dust.
Numbers assemble themselves
into something we cannot hold.

You read until the words
begin to resemble weather—
something vast
moving through the planet
without permission.

As if the earth itself
were speaking
in a language
too large to finish hearing.

The trouble is scale.

A mind evolved
to follow a trail through woods,
to read the small script
of leaf and feather,

is suddenly asked
to carry glaciers melting,
cities burning,
entire peoples reduced
to numbers
beside a plate of toast.

A goldfinch settles briefly
on the fencepost.
A towhee scratches in the leaves
with a seriousness
no government could imitate.

The kettle lifts
its thin breath of steam.
Light reaches the table—
quiet arrangements
of an ordinary life.

Wind moves through trees
with the patience
of something that has seen
civilizations before.

It does not hurry.
It does not comfort.

And the world—
without consulting us—
continues
its long
uninterrupted sentence.

MT. MITCHELL, AFTER HELENE

From up here
you would not know
how recently
the landscape was rearranged.

The ridges hold their old composure.
Spruce and fir
stand like a congregation
that has heard difficult news
and chosen not to speak.

Walk downslope
past fallen poplar and maple,
and the trail forgets
its original intention.

Root plates lifted
like trap doors in the soil,
their shallow tendrils
clutching earth and stone.

A vacant corridor opened
where wind now enters
as if someone
had kicked wide
a long-locked door
in the forest wall.

Mud the color of old brick
spread across the path

where the Parkway
surrendered
its argument
with water.

Helene passed through
like a thought
the earth
had been holding
too long.

The Swannanoa rose
without apology,
lifting culverts,
sliding fences sideways,
carrying porch steps
through the dark.

Roads learned
how provisional they were.
Bridges discovered
their fragile footing.
Trees that had practiced
a century of standing
lay down in a single day.

Yet standing here
among the deadfall
and the percolating water
reassembling its path,
small negotiations
have already begun.

Grass
working the edges
of a mudslide.

Rhododendron roots
gripping the loosened slope.

A towhee
scratching through leaves
that yesterday
lay under water.

The Blue Ridge resumes
an old conversation—
its long habit
of adjustment.

What is here
is not hope.

It is persistance:
water moving downhill,
roots gripping stone,
as if the mountains
had quietly decided
we were worth
the trouble
of one more season.

NIGHT ROAD, BLUE RIDGE

Driving late through the mountains,
as the road loosens the day,

Ahead, another car drifts—
its red lights steady,
two small rubies
stitched in the dark.

Headlights take what they can—
split-rail fences,
a pasture giving itself back to weeds,
the brief silver of a creek
slipping under a bridge.

The miles hold together
without asking anything more.
The mountains keep their distance
beyond what the lights can reach.

At home
there will be the small ceremonies:
dishes beside the sink,
coffee tin on the counter,
clothes laid over a chair.

In the morning
chickadees will riot at the feeder,
wings beating the thin air
as if the day were urgent.

I move quietly about,
setting things
gently in place—
as if the dark itself
had shown me how.

ON THE PORCH

In western North Carolina
everyone seems to have achieved
a tasteful level
of enlightenment.

They hike the same trails
every Saturday morning,
post photographs of fog
lifting off the Blue Ridge
with captions like
Grateful.

They know the names
of native wildflowers,
make excellent lentil stew,
and have strong opinions
about pollinators.

Their marriages appear stable,
held together
with heirloom tomatoes
and a shared commitment
to locally sourced optimism.

Children practicing fiddle tunes.
A golden retriever
named something philosophical
like *Thoreau.*

From a distance
their lives look finished—
like those old farmhouses

nesting easily
against the slope.

But sit long enough
on someone's porch
after supper,
when the light slips off the ridge
and the tree frogs begin
their thin evening music,

and the conversation loosens.

"Our boy hasn't called back."

"The garden never really came in
this year."

"Still waiting to hear
from FEMA."

The mountains only look smooth
from a distance.

Up close
it's ledges
and uncertain footing.

Which may be why
people keep their chairs
so close together here.

Everyone
holding themselves up

with duct tape
and good manners.

Because the mountains—
for all their calm blue distance—
are really
fault lines and pressure,
holding themselves together
one quiet inch
at a time.

And friendship turns out
to be simple:
someone admitting
I'm not as steady
as I look,

and someone else
sliding their chair closer
like a person
who understands
the terrain.

POSSIBLE SELVES

Some mornings
I sit still
long enough
to see what arrives.

Thoughts wander in
with muddy boots—
yesterday's words
tomorrow's rehearsals.

When writing
I disappear—
a line of effort
carrying me
along a narrow bridge.

The world becomes
one plank after another,
laid down
toward a distant vision.

With a friend
words come easily.
We lean beside each other
like trees in the same wind.

Alone, an inner traveler
empties his pockets,
small bright marbles
spilling everywhere.

I watch them scatter
across the floor,

one saying yes,
another turning away.

I want to gather them.
keep only the one
that may be mine.

But the self
is not a single stone
carried through the years.

It is a landscape
with many paths,
each one true
while your feet are on it,

Each one leading
a little farther
into the open country
you are becoming.

MORNING CONTEMPLATION

Mornings on the French Broad
before anyone else,
I sit in the canoe
and let it drift.

Shrubs along the bank
moving in the breeze,
the small click of the lanyard
against my vest.

I look at my hands,
tendons shifting
on the paddle,
and for a moment
they are unfamiliar.

The boat noses forward.
Reeds brush together—
a dry stitching.
Rhododendron crowds the far shore.
A rock lifts the current
into a slow turn.

Everything holds—
then a pause opens,
not thought
but something felt.

Water moving.
Light laying itself down.

For a moment

It feels enough
to be carried
a little farther downstream.

AN ORDINARY MOMENT

We're told to make something of our lives—
as if it were a casserole
we're bringing to a potluck
where everyone is judging the seasoning.

Meaning, purpose, legacy—
the big three,
lined up like motivational speakers
with wireless microphones.

Meanwhile, a Tuesday afternoon arrives—
sunlight on the counter,
a book on the desk,
your body leaning slightly
toward another cup of coffee.

Not a TED Talk,
not the heroic arc—
with opening and pivot,
just a small, unmarketable instant
refusing to mean more than itself.

And we get nervous.
We start searching—
is this leading somewhere?
will there be a takeaway?

Because staying here
feels like being trapped
in a room with no doors—
even if the room

has a sofa
and excellent lighting.

So we fidget.
Invent futures.
Anything to avoid admitting
this might be enough—
a bright, ordinary moment
we keep trying
to upgrade.

PRESENCE

Morning air
moves through
leaf and lung—
boundaries give way.

White cloud
shouldering blue,
redbud along the slope
entering its brief declaration.

Stillness under it—
not hidden,
just unattended.

A continuous,
untroubled passing.

Edges undo—
boundaries thinning
as water finds its way.

ROAN MOUNTAIN

At Carvers Gap
morning does not arrive all at once.

Fog moves in,
settling its weight
across the balds,
along the narrow cut
of the Appalachian Trail,
where it disappears
even when marked.

Catawba rhododendron
holds the slopes in green walls.
In June, hillsides lift into bloom—
now only leaf
beaded with water.

Cairns stand—
stone on stone,
small agreements with distance.
Still, the trail dissolves.
Each step found underfoot.

Wind moves through heath—
blueberry, laurel—
branches tightening
at the ankles.
Beneath them,
ramps push through last year's leaves,
their sharp scent
kept close to ground.

There are places now
you cannot go.
Side trails closed—
signs nailed to posts,
edges blunt as boards.
After Helene,
sections given back
to slope and water.
Bridges taken.
Footing loosened
beyond repair.

Fog shifts.
A ridge appears—
withdraws.

For a moment
you stand without direction—
no past step visible,
no next one certain.

A clearing
that does not hold.
A view
already closing.

And still
something in you leans forward,
as if the way continues
through what cannot be seen,

an opening
not yet found.

A breeze passes.
A cairn emerges—
one stone, then another.

You move—
guest of a new season,
taking the offered step,
not knowing.

FATE IN FLIGHT

I am sitting in an airport chair,
guarding my backpack with one boot,
eating a muffin of such indeterminate flavor
it might reasonably be classified as beige.

A man next to me is eating yogurt
with the concentration of a surgeon,
and a woman is scrolling her phone
as though the meaning of life
might be hiding between advertisements.

Across from me sits a woman
reading a paperback upside down
until she realizes
and corrects the problem
with admirable dignity.

She could be the love of my life,
though this possibility is complicated
by the fact that she is currently
wearing a neck pillow shaped like a smiling dinosaur.
And I am busy composing emails
I will later regret sending.

When our zone is called, we will stand
forming that slow, obedient river
of carry-ons and mild impatience.
She will turn left down the aisle
while I turn right,
two planets choosing different orbits.

Still, stranger things have happened—
so why not here,
between the tourist kiosk
and a carpet patterned
to disguise either coffee stains
or existential dread.

We would understand instantly
that we were meant to grow old together,
to wear Patagonia jackets,
argue about thermostat settings,
pretend we enjoy each other's in-laws.

Instead, I am scrolling headlines
about construction problems on I-26.
And she is Googling something
with the intense frown
reserved for assembling furniture.

While she adjusts her compression socks,
I take a final bathroom break
before searching my pockets
for the boarding pass
I have checked six times already.

We shuffle down the jet bridge
like survivors of a very polite train wreck—
two lives that might have merged
now choosing separate seats,

United only by the firm belief
that these overhead bins
will not hold
our luggage.

CLIMBING LOOKING GLASS

You start where it seems
you could walk—
rock leaning just enough
to ask for attention.

The stone has its own ideas.
What looks like a step
tilts away.
Your foot learns to feel
before it trusts.

There is no hurry.
A hand finds something small
and keeps it.
You move
because you can.

Higher, the wall
begins to notice you.
A breeze comes up from below—
the valley's gentle menace.

You follow a line
that isn't drawn,
just found
by the next hold,
the next step.

Somewhere in the middle
you understand
this is about moving
with what is given—
this knob of granite,
this breath.

Steeper now.
No space to argue.
Only the quiet
of choosing balance
over strength.

Then it eases—
as if the mountain
has said enough.

You walk the last wide stone
upright,
blueberries low to the ground,
holding afternoon light.

Below, the forest
folds into itself.
Wind moves through it.

You don't need to say
you've arrived.
The rock has already
let you go.

THE FRENCH BROAD RIVER

The river doesn't keep a season
but passes through—
a long sentence of water revising its clauses.

Spring comes as release:
snow loosens in the high places;
what was held becomes motion—
a brown-green urgency
under the first indecisions of bud,
each twig trying its leaf-language,
banks leaning in to listen—
sap rising—
an argument trees cannot refuse.

By summer the river remembers weight:
dust and pollen settle,
eddies hold, turn,
foam writes temporary borders
where tributaries enter—
each small water insisting on its name
before being taken.
Heat presses down.
Birds withdraw to shade.
The current continues
its low work of carrying.

Then fall—
not ending but deepening:
red arguing with gravity,
amber holding light too long,
orange a brief permission—

a bridge that will not last.
Then water rises past its usual terms,
takes fences, steps, the shaped edge of the bank,
carries what seemed settled
into motion again,
taking leaf after leaf
into continuation.

Winter strips things back:
distance returns,
dark lines cut through land,
white stone speaks
where it was always present—
the river made legible again,
taking more than it should—
or exactly what it could—
the banks revised,
the sentence continuing.

The year turns in adjustments,
each season correcting the last.
The river never the same,
never other—
not an answer
but motion—
given to gravity,
to weather;
roads loosening at their edges,
bridges remembering what they cross,
names thinning on a map—
all of it
carried downstream.

FRENCH BROAD IN SPRING

In early spring
the river loosens its voice—
not loud, but certain—
under the soft tips of red maple,
past the pale stars of serviceberry
just opening.

Along the banks,
trout lily mottles the ground,
bloodroot lifts its brief white lantern,
foamflower gathers
small constellations in shade.

The water runs with remembering—
snowmelt,
the long patience of ice.
It carries it forward.

FRENCH BROAD IN SUMMER

Summer holds—
sycamores lifting pale limbs
into the heat,
their bark catching light
without asking.

Milkweed in the fields beyond,
butterfly weed burning orange,
coneflower steady at the center
as goldfinches pass through.

Dust enters the river
as everything does—
worked into its slow turning
around stone,
through the small mouths of creeks,
arriving without announcement.

Birdsong thins at noon.
Even the towhee falls quiet.

The banks wait.
The current continues.
Everything listens.

FRENCH BROAD IN FALL

Autumn—
the great letting go—
sourwood and black gum
flaring red,
tulip poplar loosening
its yellow coins
into the drift.

The river keeps nothing.
It carries
leaf, shadow,
a brief brightness at the surface
and lets them go.

Light lengthens.
Banks come clear—
their bones of root and stone
laid bare.

FRENCH BROAD IN WINTER

A stripping back to terms more nearly final—
distance returns.

Frost holds the margins.
Leaves gone to ground;
the eye follows what was buried:
dark cuts through the land—
water, root, the old roadbed—
white stone speaking up
where it was always present.

The river made legible again,
its channels laid open—
as if clarity were only this:
what remains
after the world
stops trying to soften it.

LIGHT MOVING THROUGH CURRENT

Each moment carries something—
light moving through current
on the trout-rich Tuckasegee.

Most pass
without announcement—
days loosening,
slipping downstream.

What matters arrives quietly—
a turn in the current,
mist lifting from the valley.

You remember hard crossings—
cold coming fast,
fear tightening,
water over your boots.

And the losses—
faces thinning into distance,
voices letting go,
a name in another room.

Still, the days go on—
poplar holding shade,
stones keeping their place,
light moving leaf to leaf.

Each day
takes light
and releases it—
nothing held
long enough to stay.

LITTLE TENNESSEE GREENWAY

The current knows
more than I do.
It draws me into the channel
like a thought
I don't need to finish.

The water
takes the shape of the banks,
gathers what falls—
leaf, twig—
and lets it go.

In the drift
I forget
what I was trying to be.

Balanced in the narrow hull,
the mind grows quiet—
a wood duck
settling into shade.

The river goes on
without arriving.

Nothing held back,
nothing to become—
only this passing
that leaves no trace.

SELF-IMPROVEMENT, ASHEVILLE STYLE

It begins with a low-grade suspicion—
you've failed to become
the person this place
was designed to improve.

A voice keeps insisting
this isn't enough.
Not the filtered light
over the Blue Ridge Mountains,
not the curated calm
of a small, intentional life.

You have done the right things—
downsized, simplified,
purchased objects that suggest
a relationship to stillness:

a hand-thrown mug,
a meditation cushion,
a water bottle large enough
to imply seriousness of purpose.

You read books
about presence, about awareness,
about being where you are,
which you underline carefully.

Yet someone is always
becoming more authentic—
a man with a beard
explaining fermentation,

a woman in linen
carrying collected works
of Emily Dickinson.

Meanwhile the feeling
remains—
like a draft in a house
no renovation can correct.

It tells you fulfillment
is just outside the frame—
after the next meditation workshop,
the next chair yoga session,
the next subtle recalibration
of the self.

Meanwhile,
whatever might have been enough
waits quietly—
unbranded,
unimproved:

light through rhododendron,
a wren making spirited demands,
the Swannanoa gliding over serene pools.

And sometimes,
when the breweries close
and your devices
have stopped offering upgrades—

you notice
the mountains have not
taken a single step
toward enlightenment.

The voice persists—
preferring you dissatisfied,

rather than risk
the embarrassment
that nothing was wrong
with you
to begin with.

QUIETING THE INNER VOICE

On a morning along the New River
before traffic finds the 194 bridges,
the river moves.

An inner voice
tries its old habit—
building small fences,
standing apart.

Fog lifts—
just enough for the banks
to return.

A kingfisher—
one clean line—
gone.

The current widens.
It has always known
the way.

On the ridge,
spruce holding night,
light comes slowly—
branch to branch.

No need to follow.
No need to know.

Just this—
when the inner voice
lets go.

TABLE ROCK, SECOND PITCH

Dusty goes first,
taking his time with the overhang,
trying it again.

I stand below,
rope running through my hands,
feeling him more than seeing—
a small tug,
a pause,
then movement.

The sun sits just above the ledge.
I lift a hand
to watch him find the hold
he trusts—
too small
until it isn't.

For a moment
he stays there,
weight shifting,
looking out
over what drops away
as if to take something in
he'll carry down.

Then he's gone—
over the lip,
out of sight.

I wait for the rope to ease,
for his voice to come down,
simple as always:
"On belay."

When I reach him
we stand on the ledge
without speaking,
the rock still warm
through our shoes.

FIVE FALLS, CHATTOOGA RIVER

We had run enough river
to trust ourselves
a little too much.

Five drops in a row,
one decision after another,
no recess.

At Hole in the Wall,
Clark goes in early—
just off line
enough to be claimed.

His boat slips downstream
like it has better plans.
Clark stays
in the river's argument
with gravity.

We watch him rise,
disappear,
rise again—
a lesson in hydraulics
no one wants.

Someone throws a rope—
a bright arc of hope—
he can't take hold.

And then someone else
goes in after him.

No speech,
no plan—
just a body
choosing.

For a second
it's two lives
in the same problem.
Then the river, not sentimental,
loosens just enough
to let them go.

Clark is
struggling for breath,
negotiating with oxygen
like a man
rethinking his priorities.

He vomits—
which feels about right,
a small offering
to whatever keeps score.

We gather boats,
check straps,
adjust helmets—
the rituals of people
who continue.

Because stopping
would take
a different kind of courage.

At the end
we call it
a "good experience"—
which means
nothing worse happened.

The river keeps moving,
unimpressed,
already forgetting us,

while we retell it
until the edges smooth out—
until the moment
it could have gone otherwise
is harder to find.

FAITHFUL TO WHAT ENDURES

There is a way a person comes to be,
not by fitting parts together,
nor by instructions,
but by being drawn out slowly,
like gravel settling into its grade,
each stone finding where it must rest.

There is no blueprint for becoming.
No video titled *How to Assemble Yourself Without Crying*.
No hex key, no pictogram of a smiling figure
with all the parts finally aligned.
Only a warning label
we assume is meant for someone else.

When we were young, we were pliable.
The self stretched easily—
toward whatever called.
We bent toward approval,

twisted into someone else's dream,
mistook adaptability for truth.
We thought this was how life worked.

It felt like wisdom.

Then came hurt.
Not dramatically.
Nothing that announced itself as a turning point.
Just enough to train the mind
to hesitate—
to praise carefully,
to defer, adjust, brace.

We told ourselves we absorbed it well.
But the damage knew how to whisper.
It hid in our posture,
In the way we flinched at praise,
In how we mistook armor
For character.

We believed we were durable,
Though we were hardening.
Confusing weight with depth,
Prudence with wisdom,
Cynicism with gravity.
Rusting like a weathered hinge
Insisting it can still swing.

So we arrive at the edge of ourselves,
Asking whether this is who we are
Or only who we learned to be.
A montage of old scripts,
Ornamental scars,
Principles gone inflexible with age,
Illusions polished until they shine.

We no longer have the ease of youth.
Yet we can claim a steadier strength
Less elastic, more load-bearing.
Creaky, but still able
To gauge what matters.

To stand inside the exact outline
we have made.
To inhabit the shape honestly.
And to learn, at last,
how to be faithful
to what endures.

BACKYARD OAK

The oak in my field
is running an underground economy—
fungi trading minerals for sugar,
2,000 species checking in and out
like it's a long-term rental.

It stands there
letting things pass through—
light, water, time,
the occasional squirrel
having an existential crisis.

I contemplate the tree
while my consciousness invents
problems and regrets
and a plan
to reorganize my life
sometime next week.

The oak, meanwhile,
shimmers, then
drops a leaf—
a quiet transaction
with the breeze.

If I were less attached
to being "someone,"
would anything fall apart?

The oak doesn't say.
It continues

its slow collaborations
with earth and sky

as I stand here
trying to upgrade consciousness—
more calm, fewer glitches.
Then something loosens—
not much.
A small unfastening.

Enough to stand here
without improving it.
Enough to let the leaf fall.

SERIAL KILLER, BLUE RIDGE

The killer is small.
Call it balsam woolly adelgid
if you want to imagine science
can soften the story
by imposing a name.

It slides its mouth into bark
like a hypodermic—
no fingerprints,
just a toxin that says:
you won't be needing water anymore.

Whole ridgelines go gray.
Not the dignified gray
of weathered barns
but the gray—
of ghost forests.

On Mitchell, where the air thins
and nothing expects betrayal,
the killer —
undertakes its careful work,
injecting silence
into the circulatory system
of a mountain.

But the young don't die.
They stand there,
as if waiting their turn—
and then don't take it.

Something in them
declines the script.

Resistance,
which sounds heroic
until you realize
it's the mountain
learning to say no.
And the forest—
turns out to have
its own slow revenge—
Predators arrive.
Parasites sign on.

The ecosystem,
begins to close ranks.
No speeches.
Just pressure applied
in a thousand small ways
until the killer
becomes the hunted.

Up there now,
if you walk long enough,
you'll see it—
the dead still standing
like testimony.

Beneath them
the young firs
rising through the evidence—
green verdicts
refusing to cooperate
in the narrative
we had written
for their extinction.

BLUEBIRD AT THE DOOR

I stood behind the glass-paned door
like a man not wishing to interrupt
a conversation already underway—
wrens fussing, sparrows bickering,
finches polite as churchgoers
at the feeder on the deck.

Then he arrived—
not for the seed (he has better tastes)
but for the air itself
or for the look of things.

He lit first on the feeder,
dismissed it,
glided over to the railing,
then—bold as a deacon with collection plate—
perched on the door handle.

He surveyed—yard, gravel drive,
the fence line where he has held forth
whatever claims a bluebird stakes
in a world that keeps slipping
out from under ownership.

Sunlight dressed him—
red breast a fine waistcoat,
blue shoulders carrying it off
with no hint of vanity.

He sang then,
not to summon, not to warn,
but as if to say
the morning favored him.

He looked up at me—
once, twice—
and I wondered
if I had passed inspection
or failed to matter.

Down he went for insects,
Not our offerings,
then rose again to measure the yard,
the fence line, the air.

Out back he has a home—
we nailed together
thinking ourselves generous—
and a mate he courted
who judged it fit.

They lined it with twigs, moss,
whatever the season provided—
and went about their business
without consultation.

This regal fellow
came close enough
to make a neighbor of me,
paused just long enough
for us to share the morning.

He left on some errand
I don't pretend to know—
before either of us
had to say more than was needed.

WHAT REMAINS

We expect life to be a bright sequence—
every moment charged with potential,
something luminous tucked inside the ordinary,
waiting to be noticed, seized, held.

Most of what we live slips away
as softly as breath exhaling.
Each day is loosening its grip,
washing itself from our consciousness.

Is this how a life is meant to be,
the long effort against the small,
struggling against the trivial,
waiting for the one clear moment
that will vibrate?

Time keeps a rhythm in
long, featureless measures.
Nothing announces itself as essential.
What matters goes unnoticed.

You may remember the hard passages,
the cold pressing in,
fear tightening its grip,
the instant you thought you would fail.

And there is the quiet loss,
the slow erasing of the dead.
Faces of friends fading at the edges,
voices thinning into silence.

Even in the unremarkable hours,
life moves us forward.
No grand struggle, no sacraments, no epiphanies.
Each hour holds what it can.

Perhaps this is enough.
To move within habitual rhythms
carried by our waking routines
while our dreams keep their own account.

MEMORIES STILL WARM

The morning frost lay
over bent meadow grasses
like salt spilled from an unseen hand.
By noon it had seeped down
into dark soil and rock,
taken back into the earth's bones.

A crow lifted from the field,
a torn scrap of night
flung upward,
gone before my mind could find
a word that would hold
for the shape of its wings.

No mason jar could keep
the life of frost from leaking out,
or crow-flight,
or the warmth passing
from one hand to another,
like water poured carefully
not to spill.

No pond asks
how long it may keep the moon.
It wrinkles the light
between cattails and fallen branches,
lets the sky take back
what was never owned.

The smell of woodsmoke
caught in a jacket sleeve,
thrumming cadence of a clawhammer banjo,

mica flashing in a creek bed
like coins no one bothered to gather.

We have no instructions
except to notice.
This is our one authority:
not to lengthen the days
nor bargain with the dark
but to choose what we carry
through the narrowing gate.

A barred owl calling
from a stand of shagbark hickory.
The furnace-warm weight
of a dog leaning against your leg,
as if you were the only solid thing in its world.

A stranger's face
suddenly open with kindness.
The sound of wind
rushing through pines
so that the whole ridge sounds like distant surf.

These we tuck
into the hidden lining of the self,
like galax leaves pressed in a book.
Not because they will last
but because they will not.

And at the end,
whenever it comes,
however quietly,
we will find memories still warm,
like embers under ash
in a stove gone dark.

I DO NOT GRIEVE FOR SUMMER

It is good to walk slowly—
to feel the ground take your weight,
to breathe what the day is carrying.

Bloodroot gone to leaf,
pink turtlehead along the bank—
ironweed, or primrose,
I don't decide.

Voices above me.
A far clap of thunder.
My legs wet with dew and sweat.
Below, the creek working itself over stone.
Birds staking their claims.
Insects stitching the warm air.

The weather turns without asking—
dust to rain,
the path darkening underfoot.
Sun flickers and goes.

The moon lifts clear of the ridge.
Stars come on, one at a time.
Days thinning now,
night holding a little longer.
A cooler breath moving through.
I do not grieve for summer.
It will return.

The trail goes on ahead—
whether or not
I keep it company.

NATURE'S LESSON

A cloud over the Black Mountains
does not keep its frame—
thinning into light,
the sky finishing
what it began.

Along the Swannanoa,
a sycamore leaf turns once
and lets the current
decide the rest—
no argument,
only the small grace
of going along.

Morning fog in the hollows
touches fence posts,
then lifts—
as if it trusted
where it's going.

A man on the graded road
stops to watch a crow
tilt into wind,
finding the place
where wing and air agree.

Here—
in the pull of water,
in grass leaning with weather—
something shows how to live:

stand long enough
to feel where it opens,
then step there—

as the leaf does,
as the cloud does,
as morning does
giving itself
to day.

80TH BIRTHDAY

Friends, like sunflowers erupting in a farmer's field,
rush to embrace me, urge that I banish regret,
seek the grace of simple things.

Shaking off aches and hesitation,
I feel the liberating communion of others.
Music and a chorus of song pulse through the room.
Toasts evoke humor (and hyperbole).

Who could turn from this World in this moment?

Yet friends depart as the sun falls beneath the Blue Ridge.

I am left to contemplate a long ago longing.
Night surrounds and swaddles.
Stars offer little consolation, my ancient eyes are blurred.
The creep of vertigo pairs with wanting to weep.

One day a shadow will hide my way.
May this morning illuminate that moment,
invest me with the fierceness of youth.

ANYTHING LEFT TO SAY?

Is there anything left to say?
We gather what remains—
not scraps, but fragments
still warm with use,
our fingers tracing
where others have touched
and adding our own small pressure.

We carry a bucket across a life,
sloshing with possibility.
It spills—
but not all loss is waste.
Some of it marks the ground,
darkening the path behind us,
a record of our passing.

We steady what we can,
not to keep it whole—
but to feel its movement,
to walk in rhythm with it.

Balance becomes the work.
Presence, the discipline—
and the gift:
less like vigilance,
more like attention widening.

We look to the heavens,
and though the stars do not answer,
they burn anyway—

their silence not refusal,
their light already arriving.

Perhaps we will end exploring,
send out one last probe—
a message in a bottle,
that something in us
refused to be still.

Or not a message at all
but a stone skipped across water—
not meant to arrive anywhere,
only to touch, again and again,
the surface that receives it.

We stand on the shore,
counting the skips—
as witness:

that something was set in motion,
that it moved with grace for a time,
that we were here—
not to last
but to enter the arc
and give it shape.

ABOUT THE AUTHOR

In his early years, Joe Beckham guided fishermen in Yellowstone Park, climbed in the Tetons, and taught courses for the North Carolina, Minnesota, and Hurricane Island Outward Bound Schools. He also earned a BA from the University of South Florida and a JD from the University of Florida.

His background in administrative law led to an appointment as Administrative Counsel to the Lieutenant Governor of Connecticut, where he helped develop programs for youthful offenders funded by the Law Enforcement Assistance Administration, including the Connecticut Wilderness School, an adaptive Outward Bound program.

Joe later joined the University of Florida's National Education Finance Project, authoring a state constitutional amendment expanding the authority of Florida's public higher education system. After teaching at the University of Pennsylvania, he moved to Florida State University in 1980 to direct the Center for Studies in Higher Education.

During a 35-year career at FSU, he became nationally recognized for research on higher education policy and law, publishing widely and teaching graduate courses in education law, policy, and finance. He retired in 2011 as a named professor and emeritus faculty member.

An advocate for greenways and trails, he helped establish Florida's first rail trail, the St. Marks Trail, and was president of the Florida Greenways and Trails Foundation. Since 2022 he's been active with the White Horse, Asheville Symphony, and Greenville's Peace Center. Relocating to Highland Farms in November 2025, he remains active with OLLI /UNCA, writes poetry, practices clawhammer banjo, and enjoys time with his grandchildren.

ABOUT THE PHOTOGRAPHER

Now in the waning years of his life and well into retirement, the relentless search for meaning and fulfillment continues to doggedly nip at his heals. Since his earliest recollections, Skip Sickler has sought solace in the outdoors. While immersed in the mountains, forests, and streams, he finds himself more centered, more alive. "It is the rekindling of the scared fire of which I am most in need— a reprieve from the daily concerns of life in a bustling world of people, cars, and other modern distractions."

Years ago, Skip was moved by a passage written by Aldo Leopold in his classic work on the conservation of the natural resources, *A Sand County Almanac*: "We reached the old wolf in time to watch the green fire dying in her eyes. I realized then, and have known ever since, that there was something new to me in those eyes—something known to her and to the mountain." Skip continues to search for the essence of "the green fire," the mystery and magic of life. It is this sense of wonder he continues to cultivate within himself as an artist. After all, art is only a means of seeing. Sigurd Olson wrote, "Only when one comes to listen, only when one is aware and still, can things be seen and heard." Skip's photography helps him look more closely, more intensely, more soulfully, more intentionally at the world and his relationship to it. The translation of these feelings into a visual image is his challenge of creating impact and meaning as an artist and, ultimately, to have an influence on viewers' reactions to his work.

Skip began photography in 1971 when he received a camera for Christmas. A camera was his constant companion while working as a National Park Service Ranger, as a wilderness guide/instructor with Outward Bound, and as a trainer for various groups and teams. Skip considers himself still a student and continually seeks to see the world around him with "fresh eyes." He invites you to join him in the protection and preservation of wild areas, where nature lives and survives by the ingrained rules written in its DNA and the natural processes that have shaped our fragile blue spaceship, planet Earth.

www.ingramcontent.com/pod-product-compliance
Lightning Source LLC
Chambersburg PA
CBHW052017150726
47999CB00004B/1696